A pika watches for danger from a rocky lookout.

ANIMALS OF THE
HIGH MOUNTAINS

by Judith E. Rinard

BOOKS FOR YOUNG EXPLORERS
NATIONAL GEOGRAPHIC SOCIETY
COPYRIGHT © 1989 NATIONAL GEOGRAPHIC SOCIETY   LIBRARY OF CONGRESS CIP DATA: P. 32

IN THE HIGH MOUNTAINS of North America, a grizzly bear searches for food in the summer. Even in summer, the mountains are cold and windy. The bear needs heavy fur to keep warm.

In this book, you will meet mountain animals all over the world. The map shows the continents where they live. What animals do you think you will find?

THE WORLD

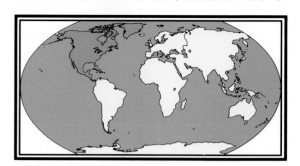

In North America, a marmot looks
down from a high, rocky ledge.
If it spots an enemy such as a wolf
or a bear, it will whistle a warning.
Marmots nearby will take cover.

This marmot peeks out
from the doorway of its home
in the rocks. When danger has
passed, it will go look for food.

Marmots are large relatives
of squirrels. All summer, they grow
fat by eating grasses and other small
plants. Then they hibernate, or sleep
all winter, in their cozy homes.

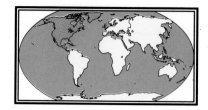

Mountain goats live on high, steep slopes. Their hooves can grip icy rocks. The hooves are split and have rubbery pads.

A female goat, or nanny, watches over her baby, called a kid. Soon after birth, it can stand and jump. This kid leaps playfully. Its thick coat keeps it warm. High up and safe from most enemies, the goats find tiny plants to eat.

Pounce! A hungry bobcat leaps
after a hare hidden in the snow.
The bobcat is a hunter, like
some other mountain animals.

Out jumps a snowshoe hare.
It races for its life. Furry pads
on its feet act like little
snowshoes. They keep the hare
from sinking into the snow.

A mountain lion watches
from its rocky den. It hunts
deer and smaller animals.

In late summer, a pika gathers small plants and dries them in the sun. It piles up this food near its den and has plenty to eat all winter long.

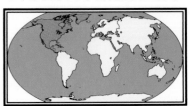

Winter is a hard time
for many animals.
Snow covers the ground.
A bighorn sheep must dig
with its hooves and horns
to uncover grasses to eat.

With its long claws,
a grizzly bear lifts a rock
to find insects. The bear
eats insects, berries, fish,
and other food all summer
and gets fat. In winter,
it sleeps, living off its fat.

A guanaco stands alert on a windy mountain in South America. It eats the grasses there.

ANIMALS OF **SOUTH AMERICA**

A baby llama snuggles close to its mother. Vicuñas drink at a water hole. Llamas and vicuñas are cousins of guanacos. Their thick wool keeps them warm. Vicuñas can run fast to get away from enemies like wild cats. Just minutes after birth, a baby vicuña can run faster than the fastest person!

SOUTH AMERICA

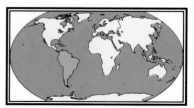

A viscacha warms itself in the sun. It may look asleep, but it is really awake. If it hears a fox or other enemy, it will leap into its home among the rocks.

Large vultures called condors soar on their broad wings. These birds sail on warm air that rises up the sides of mountains.

Condors see well. They mostly eat dead animals that they can spot from high in the sky.

SOUTH AMERICA

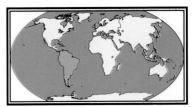

In Africa, furry little
rock hyraxes peep out
from their homes
high among the rocks.
How many do you see?
When leopards or eagles
come near, the hyraxes
run to hiding places.

ANIMALS OF **AFRICA**

A black eagle carries a twig in its beak for its nest.
Later, the eagle will use its feet to carry food to its chicks.

A family of rock hyraxes huddles together. Adults take
turns caring for the young. A female mountain gorilla
cradles her baby as it drinks her milk. Mountain gorillas
live in high forests. They are shy and gentle animals.

AFRICA

Two little antelopes called
klipspringers nuzzle each other. Only
the male has horns. Klipspringers
can escape quickly from enemies
by springing from rock to rock.

A klipspringer stands on tiptoe.
It walks, stands, and jumps
on the tips of its tiny hooves.
It can land safely with all four feet
on a rock smaller than a doorknob!

ANIMALS OF **EUROPE**

Ibexes live on rocky slopes in the high mountains of Europe. They can race up and down steep, icy cliffs without slipping.

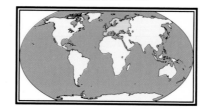

Who's there? An alert
chamois looks down
a snowy ridge.
If alarmed, this goatlike
animal will run and leap
down the slope.
Its legs act like springs
to help it land safely.

Mountain sheep called
mouflons stay warm
in woolly coats.

26

Male sheep, or rams, have long curving horns. The oldest and strongest have the largest horns. Rams use them to fight other rams for females.

The snow leopard lives in the high mountains of Asia. Spotted fur helps it hide from its prey. At night, it keeps its nose warm by wrapping its long tail around its face.

ANIMALS OF **ASIA**

ASIA

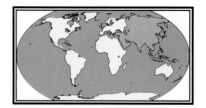

A giant panda munches bamboo.
The panda lives in forests
in the mountains of China.
Furry snow monkeys in Japan
hug each other for warmth.
All over the world, animals are
at home in the mountains.

An ibex finds its way down a rocky mountain. Its hard-edged hooves have pads that grip the rock like suction cups.

COVER: An expert climber, a mountain goat looks out from a high ridge.

Published by

The National Geographic Society, Washington, D. C.
Gilbert M. Grosvenor,
    President and Chairman of the Board
Melvin M. Payne, Thomas W. McKnew,
    Chairmen Emeritus
Owen R. Anderson, *Executive Vice President*
Robert L. Breeden, *Senior Vice President,*
    Publications and Educational Media

Prepared by

The Special Publications and School Services Division
Donald J. Crump, *Director*
Philip B. Silcott, *Associate Director*
Bonnie S. Lawrence, *Assistant Director*

Staff for this book

Jane R. McGoldrick, *Managing Editor*
Jane H. Buxton, *Consulting Managing Editor*
Charles M. Kogod, *Illustrations Editor*
Cinda Rose, *Art Director*
Marianne R. Koszorus, *Associate Art Director*
Rebecca Lescaze, *Researcher*
Jody Bolt, Joseph F. Ochlak, *Map Editors*
Sharon Kocsis Berry, *Illustrations Assistant*
Susan A. Bender, Catherine G. Cruz,
    Marisa J. Farabelli, Lisa A. LaFuria,
    Sandra F. Lotterman, Eliza C. Morton,
    Jennie H. Proctor, Dru McLoud Stancampiano,
    Staff Assistants

Engraving, Printing, and Product Manufacture

George V. White, *Director,* and Vincent P. Ryan,
    Manager, Manufacturing and Quality Management
David V. Showers, *Production Manager*
Kathleen M. Cirucci, *Production Project Manager*
Carol R. Curtis, *Senior Production Staff Assistant*

Consultants

Dr. James M. Dietz, University of Maryland,
    Dr. George E. Watson, St. Albans School,
    Washington, D. C., *Scientific Consultants*
Peter L. Munroe, *Educational Consultant*
Dr. Lynda Bush, *Reading Consultant*

Illustrations Credits

Chase Swift (cover, 11 upper); Stephen J. Krasemann/DRK PHOTO (1); Rick McIntyre (2–3, 6); Kenneth W. Fink/NATIONAL AUDUBON SOCIETY COLLECTION, PHOTO RESEARCHERS, INC. (4–5); Larry Ulrich/DRK PHOTO (5); ANIMALS ANIMALS/David C. Fritts (6–7); Alan & Sandy Carey (7); Jeanne Drake (8 upper); Michael S. Quinton (8 lower); Daniel J. Cox (9); Thomas Kitchin/TOM STACK & ASSOCIATES (10); Dick Canby/DRK PHOTO (11 lower); Erwin & Peggy Bauer (12–13); ANIMALS ANIMALS/Zig Leszczynski (14); Günter Ziesler/BRUCE COLEMAN LTD (15, 20 upper); François Gohier (16, 17 lower, 31); © Günter Ziesler/PETER ARNOLD, INC. (17 upper, 18–19); Frank S. Balthis (20 lower); Peter Veit/DRK PHOTO (21); ANIMALS ANIMALS/Arthur Gloor (22–23); Anthony Bannister/OXFORD SCIENTIFIC FILMS (23); Eric Dragesco/BRUCE COLEMAN INC (24–25); © Manfred Danegger/PETER ARNOLD, INC. (26); ANIMALS ANIMALS/Stefan Meyers (26–27); ANIMALS ANIMALS/Bruce M. Wellman (27); E. R. Degginger/FOLIO INC. (28–29); Terry Domico/EARTH IMAGES (30); Leonard Lee Rue III (32).

Library of Congress CIP Data

Rinard, Judith E.
    Animals of the high mountains / by Judith E. Rinard.
        p.   cm. — (Books for young explorers)
    Bibliography: p.
    Summary: Depicts mountain animals from all over the world, including the mountain lion, llama, rock hyrax, and ibex.
    ISBN 0-87044-771-8 (regular edition)
    ISBN 0-87044-776-9 (library edition)
    1. Alpine fauna—Juvenile literature.   [1. Alpine animals.]
I. Title. II. Series.
QL 113.R56 1989
599.0909'43—dc20   89-12817
                                                                CIP
                                                                AC

MORE ABOUT Animals of the High Mountains

Mountains are home to many kinds of animals, all suited to life in a harsh environment. This book features animals found at 10,000 feet or higher. Even here, on the high mountains, the terrain varies from gently rolling hills to steep, rugged peaks.

Major ranges, or chains, of high mountains around the world include the Rocky Mountains in North America, the Andes in South America, the Alps in Europe, and the Himalaya in Asia. Africa has smaller mountain ranges and some isolated high peaks.

Mountains have a great variety of climates and habitats. The higher up a mountain you climb, the lower the temperature. Snow and ice cover many mountaintops all year. At some levels, high mountains may have thick forests, such as those in Africa where the mountain gorilla lives (21).*

At the highest elevations everywhere, the climate is too cold, dry, and windy for trees to grow. The upper limit of tree growth is called the timberline. Above the timberline, only the hardiest plants survive, such as mosses, tough grasses, and low-lying shrubs .

Many high slopes have piles of broken rocks and boulders. These provide shelter and hiding places for small mammals, such as the marmot (4–5) and the pika of North America (1, 10), the viscacha of South America (16), and the rock hyrax of Africa (18–19, 20).

Near the summits of the highest mountains, living conditions are

among the harshest of any environment in the world. At times, fierce winds reach speeds greater than 100 miles an hour. Most animals that live there have warm, thick coats. Many have specialized feet that enable them to climb on rocky crags and icy cliffs.

Several kinds of hoofed mammals live on the highest slopes. They include the Rocky Mountain goat of North America (6–7), the ibex (24–25) and the chamois (26) of Europe, and the mountain sheep of North America and Europe (11, 26–27). All excellent climbers, these animals have split hooves that can spread wide apart to grip rocks like pincers. Their soft hoof pads hold like rubber to slippery rock and ice.

Most of these animals move to lower slopes in winter, but the mountain goat stays on the heights all year. It has four stomachs for digesting sparse, tough twigs. This enables it to gain every possible bit of nourishment. The goat's two-layer coat helps keep it warm. Beneath the long, shaggy outer coat is a four-inch-thick layer of short inner hair that insulates the animal.

Winter is the most difficult season for most animals. Temperatures are low, and deep snow may cover the ground. Some creatures, such as the marmot and the grizzly bear (2–3, 11), are dormant. They sleep in sheltered dens or burrows in the rocks. Others, such as the pika, stay active all winter, eating food they have stored (10).

Several animals have special adaptations for moving over deep snow and staying warm in winter. The

HANS REINHARD/BRUCE COLEMAN INC

A bird called a wallcreeper lives in mountains from Spain to Tibet. It nests as high as 18,000 feet. With its long claws, the wallcreeper clings to high, vertical cliffs. It uses its long beak to probe for insects.

snowshoe hare of North America (8) and the snow leopard of Asia (28–29) have wide, furred feet that distribute body weight as the animals travel over snow. The hare and the leopard have small ears, an adaptation that reduces heat loss.

Soaring birds, such as the black eagle of Africa (20) and the Andean condor of South America (17), are among the most successful high-mountain dwellers. The Andean condor is the largest member of the

*Numbers in parentheses refer to pages in *Animals of the High Mountains*.

One of the hardiest of mountain dwellers, the yak serves as both pack animal and provider for the people of central Asia's high regions. It supplies meat, milk for cheese and butter, hair for cloth, and hide for leather. This yak wears a pack cloth that cushions its back.

vulture family, with a wingspan of ten feet. In spite of the condor's size, its body is light because its bones are hollow. This lightness allows the bird to glide on warm air currents that rise up mountainsides. Both eagles and condors have exceptionally keen eyesight. A condor, which mainly scavenges for dead animals, can spot a guanaco carcass from as far away as five miles.

Some mountain animals have retreated to the highlands as a last sanctuary from human hunters. The mountain lion (9) and the grizzly bear once ranged widely over North America. Yet because people killed so many of these animals, they are found today mainly in high, hard-to-reach mountain country.

A few animals that live in the mountains are severely endangered today, largely because humans have hunted them for fur or for other body parts or taken over their habitats. These animals include the giant panda of China (30), the snow leopard, and the mountain gorilla.

For thousands of years, people of the high mountains have depended on animals. The Indians of the Andes in South America still rely heavily on the llama (14), which they domesticated long ago. The Indians use the llama as a pack animal to carry goods along steep trails. And they depend on the llama as a source of meat and wool. They spin the wool into yarn for clothing and rope. The hide of the llama is tanned for sandals, and its fat goes into

candles. Even the llama's dung is useful: It is dried and burned as fuel for cooking and for heating.

The llama and its relatives, the guanaco (12–13) and the vicuña (15), are members of the camel family. They are well adapted to high elevations, where there is less oxygen than at lower levels. The animals have blood rich in red cells. The extra red cells increase the blood's oxygen-carrying capacity.

The people who live in the high mountains of central Asia depend on the yak (shown on this page). This powerful yet agile animal is a member of the cattle family. An amazingly hardy pack animal, it can survive temperatures as low as minus 40°F. The shaggy yak provides milk for milk products; hair for cloth; meat; and hide.

Look at a map of the world to see where the major groups of high mountains are found. Are there mountains near where you live? Do you know what animals live there?

On your next trip to a zoo, find some animals of the high mountains. Look closely at their bodies, and try to see how their fur, feet, and other features help them survive in their natural surroundings.

ADDITIONAL READING

Book of Mammals, 2 vols. (Washington, D. C., National Geographic Society, 1981). Ages 8 and up.

The First Book of Mountains, by Frances Smith. (New York, Franklin Watts, Inc., 1964). Ages 8 and up.

Mountain Animals, by Tony Long. (New York, Harper & Row, Publishers, 1971). Family reference.

Mountain Wildlife, by Richard Perry. (Harrisburg, Pa., Stackpole Books, 1981). Family reference.